Bitch, Pitch, and Get Rich

(Success at the Tip of Your Tongue)

LEE PAUL

iUniverse, Inc.
Bloomington

Bitch, Pitch, and Get Rich
(Success at the Tip of Your Tongue)

iUniverse books may be ordered through booksellers or by contacting:

iUniverse
1663 Liberty Drive
Bloomington, IN 47403
www.iuniverse.com
1-800-Authors (1-800-288-4677)

ISBN: 978-1-4502-9321-1 (pbk)
ISBN: 978-1-4502-9323-5 (cloth)
ISBN: 978-1-4502-9322-8 (ebk)

Printed in the United States of America

iUniverse rev. date: 3/16/11

About the Author

Balancing an early interest in both science and the arts, Lee Paul grew up in Brooklyn, New York, went to college in Marietta, Ohio, worked for oil companies in Williston, North Dakota, and Falfurrias, Texas, acted in the theater in Cincinnati, Ohio and Charlotte North Carolina, and was an officer in the Air Force in Reno, Nevada and King Salmon, Alaska. With the chance to travel extensively, he finally found his own personal "Yellow Brick Road" which led him to Hollywood, and a career in Television and Films. After 25 years and over a 100 appearances "on camera" in episodic series and commercials, his deep interest in life and living has prompted him to extract some of the important lessons gleaned from an insatiable curiosity about all around him. Always asking why, or why not, he wanted to learn more and constantly attempted to increase his vision and knowledge. Lee found there were others he knew, who longed to improve and grow as individuals as well, but were not sure of the road to take, or the path to follow. Their uncertainty proved the inspiration for **"Bitch, Pitch and get Rich."**

For those who peruse its pages, he offers a sincere wish that they find the inspiration and direction to make themselves a most successful part of this fascinating and challenging world. Practice the principles and find:

"Success at the tip of your Tongue"

I would like to dedicate this book
to the memory of my father, Leon J. Kroll,
who was one of the great raconteurs,

to Mr. David Blossom, who was instrumental
in my education and my many travels,

and to the confidants and acquaintances who
have so enriched my life.

May I also extend a special thanks
to the following friends
who have given suggestions and support
in the writing of this book:

William Pugsley
Sterling von Franck
John Nolan
William D. Stern

and my wife, Kathy Kroll, without whose
motivation and direction, this book would
never been completed.

PREFACE

Almost 20 years ago I wrote **"Bitch, Pitch and get Rich"** a self-help book with a different approach. I used a number of personal stories to underscore the lessons to be practiced for individual enrichment and development.

In these present economic times, the lessons and exercises outlined in the book those many moons ago, have become even more relevant and significant today. In fact, I find myself reaffirming the simple but powerful strategies highlighted in **"Bitch, Pitch and get Rich"** to help me focus my own thinking and outlook today.

To have the confidence and self-esteem to tackle life's obstacles and not only succeed, but also enjoy the challenge, seems a worthy and meaningful goal. **"Bitch, Pitch and get Rich"** was written with the assurance that those who practice the easy, yet powerful ideas advanced between its covers will both prosper and find their own personal path to success.

Lee Paul
Woodland Hills, CA
2011

INTRODUCTION

We all want to reach the top of the mountain, whether we have actually seen it or thought about it. It's a noble goal and we must train our mind, body and spirit, and work hard and well, to achieve it.

But this book is not only about achieving the heights, it is about the byways, so often missed by those who only scramble for the top, as well. It is also about those who look only at their feet, lest they fall along the way.

Always recall that to falter is not to fail.

Some of us are natural climbers, while others of us dread losing our grip or our direction. And so it is in life and in living as well. The joy of discovery, the challenge of curiosity, and the thrill of self improvement, are often dulled by the fear of failure or the lack of confidence needed to succeed. **Do you:**

A. Have trouble expressing yourself?

B. Find you can't remember things?

C. Feel afraid to speak up?

D. Dislike the sound of your voice?

E. Find yourself being verbally pushed around?

F. Tend to find life dull and boring?

G. Resent being ignored?

H. Honestly feel poor in pocket and in spirit?

If you relate to one or more of these conditions, this book is for you.

In it you will find the practical answers and discover the maxims that will allow you to reap the riches that life has to offer, and help you reach your fullest potential.

You can change; you can improve; you can excel. All it takes is a little time, effort and concentration, and the willingness to apply the well-worn principles underlined in this book.

A little effort on your part coupled with the life lessons revealed in the numerous "Show-Biz" stories in **"Bitch, Pitch and get Rich"** will work wonders.

"Super Selling" scenarios sprinkled throughout these pages, will ensure your success.

So read a little, laugh a little, and learn a lot about your self, your goals, and your potential for success. Through escapades that cover sixty years and span the continent, you'll share the good times and the bad, the highlights and the lows, and find, somewhere in between, the joys of living life to the full.

Together we will share the exhilaration of truly being involved with everything and everyone around us, and hopefully challenge ourselves to new heights of achievement and accom-plishment. If you apply yourself to the principles underscored in **"BITCH, PITCH and get RICH"** you will:

1. increase your memory

2. expand your vocabulary

3. improve your speaking voice

4. develop verbal confidence

5. be encouraged to reach your fullest potential personally and financially

In the end, you, too, will discover the rewards of

"SUCCESS AT THE TIP OF YOUR TONGUE"

CHAPTER SUMMARY

Topics covered:

Riches of the spirit, as well as the wallet
The passing of time and friends
What it is to be truly **Rich**

On "The Sting" set with famous photographer
Marie Cosindas, Universal Studios, 1972

CHAPTER 1

"Memory and The Gift of Gab"

Some lucky people learn it, but unfortunately few are born with it. Those are the natural born story tellers, who know how to start, and when to stop, talking.

The fine art of learning to talk effectively is also the fine art of learning when to "Fermer la bouche." The French say that when they mean, *close your mouth*.

And always have a good exit line!

Remember, before you start telling a joke, no matter how funny you think it is, you better know the punch line. So, one of the first steps is start working on your memory.

**Organization is part of memory,
so let's get organized**

A good way to start is to jot things down in a note pad or begin carrying a small voice recorder. At first it is a bit of a pain, but how many times have you said "I heard the greatest joke today, but I can't remember how it ends."

Of course if you are like my father you won't have to make lists. He was one of the great spinners of tales, and weavers of dreams, you'd ever be lucky enough to meet. He could hold captive the attention and "imagination" of a room of people for hours at a time.

The operative word here is "Details"

That's what you have to start training yourself to store in those little gray cells. Details are the adjectives of life. How cold was it? It was so cold your breath just froze in front of your face!

Details!

They put color in the cheeks of your love, and because detail adds so much to the visual picture, helps you remember who your love is.

So while details help you enrich the texture and fabric of your story, to the delight of your listeners, they also help you remember the story in the first place.

Start training your eyes and ears to recognize and remember the **"Details,"** the colors of life.

I started this chapter by saying you must remember how the joke ends, and be sure to have a good exit line. Here's one example from my father's memory I was fortunate to hear one warm and sultry evening in Brooklyn:

It had been a blistering hot day that summer, and even when sun came down, the humidity was still killing. Your shirt stuck to your skin like a wet dishtowel. We had all the windows open, as well as the door to the hall, to let what little breeze there was find its way into our fifth floor flat. You could hear his voice echoing down the long dark hallway.

Remember the Details!

It was the thirties in Chicago, and at the time, my father was a "writer" in a bookmaking operation on the east side. Working in a wire room, he was one of the guys that put up the names of the tracks, the horses and the odds on the blackboards. Though my father had never finished grade school, he never forgot anything, and had this terrifically neat hand writing.

Around lunch time, the "nice guys" decide to send out for deli, and sent my father around the corner to pick up the sandwiches.

While he's gone, the joint is raided, cops everywhere...

As he returned with 6 pastrami, 4 egg salad, and a liverwurst on rye, a cop at the door stopped him, said a raid was in progress, and wanted to know what he was doing there?

Without batting an eye, my father said "You mean this is a real bookie joint? I'm just delivering an order some guy called in. I guess they're too busy to eat. How about a couple of pastrami on the house?" He gave him the order, and beat it.

Always know when to get out of Dodge!

In an ironic twist of fate, many years later I found myself playing Robert Shaw's bodyguard, in the Academy Award winning film, "The Sting." Ironic, because if you remember the movie, the main action took place in a wire room of a bookie joint in Chicago.

Con men and grifters in the depression of the 30's. I was not a "writer" like my father, but a garbage man (body guard) for Robert Shaw's role of Lonnegan in the film.

Still the coincidences between my father's real life story, and my make-believe acting role in the movie, were remarkable.

I am not about to dictate questions of ethics or morality, but even in the few tales told so far, I'm sure you have decided my father was a bit temerarious.

Important Point

If you don't know a word, always look it up. In fact start looking up every word you read or hear that you're not familiar with. A good working knowledge of the language, as well as a broad vocabulary, is essential to developing a compelling "gift of gab."

Being able to stay on your linguistic feet while others around you are tap dancing with the truth is not only the key to survival, but to success as well.

Part of the fine art of the "Gift of Gab" is knowing what is the lie, what is the truth, and what lies between. And don't forget to listen!

How many times have you been in the middle of a conversation and realized you've forgotten what original point? Or said to yourself "Why did I start this?"

This often happens because you are so busy talking that, you forget to listen as well! And even if the other person were allowed to get a word in edgewise, you're too busy to hear them.

So take a deep breath, relax, and take the time to listen as well as talk. That is the real essence of a "Gift of Gab," and with that <u>you can sell anything,</u> including the most important asset you have, and the reason for this book:

YOURSELF

In every conversation there is an ebb and flow, a give and take, a sharing of thoughts and ideas.

Before you can start winning the battle of words,

Before you can sell an idea,

Before you can convince someone to accept your point of view, you have to be able to convince yourself!

So start really listening to yourself as you talk. Start challenging yourself by asking,

Do I believe what I'm saying?

Is what I'm saying clear and to the point?

Do I understand what I'm talking about, or is it an exercise in the futile feeble flapping of my gums?

A terrific exercise to begin strengthening your verbal skills is to:

START READING OUT LOUD

We are, very much how we sound. We all can't sound like James Earl Jones, but coming to terms with our true vocal sound, is a place to start.

Using that trusty voice recorder, start reading out loud: newspapers, magazines, even the TV Guide.

What you read is not important, but speaking up, really listening to your vocal sound, and getting used to your speaking voice is the first step toward achieving verbal confidence.

It can be quite a shock to some, when they hear themselves being played back on the voice recorder for the first time: the pauses, the stumbles, the repetition, the corrections.

Even the actual vocal quality of one's speaking voice will not be what we expected. We think we know how we sound, but how we sound to others, can be quite surprising.

Often, at first, we will not like what we hear.

I was lucky to work with James Earl Jones on his series "Paris," and to hear that deep resonate voice first hand was quite an experience. Of course almost every one remembers his voice as Darth Vader, in the "Stars Wars Trilogy", and "This Is CNN."

It is probably true that Mr. Jones was born with his magnificent vocal instrument, but it is also true that we can all improve the quality of our vocal sound if we are willing to work on it.

Once again that dirty word, work, creeps into one's reality. It is an undeniable fact, however: if you work on your voice quality, develop your vocabulary, and enhance your memory, your improved communications skills will benefit you in every endeavor you pursue.

So, how do you start to develop a better sounding speaking voice?

LEARN TO RELAX

Often we rob ourselves of whatever pleasant vocal timbre we might have or whatever vocal resonance we naturally possess by just plain tension.

Usually we are so busy talking we don't even take time to breathe. We talk as if the house was on fire. Before the voice can function easily and naturally you must be vocally relaxed with enough breath to easily say the words.

We must concentrate on vocal relaxation!

Luckily, breathing is something you don't have to think about. The body and mind work together to ensure you have enough breath to speak. You just have to give yourself enough time to <u>breathe</u>.

I don't mean those little catch-up breaths, so you can keep rattling on, but taking enough time for the body to inhale naturally.

Take the time to breathe

Without knowing it, subconsciously, we are afraid to take too much time to breathe. We are afraid the other person will jump in and start talking.

Let us assume they do. It's OK. We will get another chance to respond soon enough. Let's just hope that when we do, we have something significant to say.

But let's get back to a better sounding voice

All of us have a natural resonant pitch. It is the note, or series of notes on the musical scale, where your speaking voice functions most effectively. I might add, it is also the pitch, where your voice is its most beautiful.

Now, you don't have to be a musician, or read music, to find this natural pitch for yourself. Each person has his or her tone. It depends upon the size of the chest, and the individual qualities of the voice you were born with.

But I will tell you, the natural resonant pitch of your speaking voice will be, almost without exception, lower than the pitch you are speaking at right now.

Find your natural speaking resonance

To determine where your natural resonance lies, put your hand on your chest and start talking as you normally would. Try to sense, or feel, the vibrations in your chest cavity. Then lower the sound of your voice one tone at a time.

Keep it up until you find the tone where your speaking voice creates the most vibrations in your chest. It's a subtle difference, but you will find it.

It will be the place or level where you should now consciously try to speak. It won't happen over-night, but you will be surprised how quickly you will be able to, comfortably and naturally, train yourself to talk there.

Once you can speak at your natural resonant pitch, with out thinking about it, you will have acquired a major speaking tool. And with this knowledge, your voice will be more expressive and effective.

You will have taken a major step, in using your voice effectively. Just think about resonance as you speak.

You will forget, but you will also member

Slowly your ear will correct you, and soon you will almost demand of yourself this new-found resonance and expressiveness.

Start thinking about your vocal potential

You can improve your vocal speaking ability with practice, concentration, and discipline.

Yes, to use your mouth effectively you have to know what to say and when to say it. Just as important, however, is what you sound like, saying it.

The late, great genius, Orson Wells, epitomizes the effective use of the speaking voice. I'm sure you have your favorites, but I choose Mr. Wells primarily because of his work in radio. Who can forget his incredible broadcast of "The War of the Worlds"?

Happily some of his famous radio programs, from 1939 to 1945, are still available. They are entitled, "Theatre of the Imagination": six hours of his best radio work, illustrating how incredibly effective his voice was. The great news is that with work your voice can be as persuasive.

All of us have been endowed with the gift of speech, that is one of the primary tools that separates us from the beasts in the field. We owe it to ourselves and our progeny to accept this legacy. We must challenge ourselves to use the language with precision and clarity.

As we practice and improve, we will slowly begin to like our vocal image. Once we begin to feel comfortable with our new verbal and vocal self, we will find the confidence to do battle on every linguistic front.

CHAPTER REVIEW

Details: provide the color which triggers our remembrance, and fires the imagination of the listener.

Read out loud: listen to how your voice sounds to others. We must find the vocal resonance that allows our voice to be its expressive best.

Use the voice recorder: reviewing the conversations with friends, we will begin to critically examine what we say, and how we say it.

Watch yourself in a mirror: Look closely at yourself to find the truth. You will learn to like what you see and say.

Take time and stay relaxed: allow the voice to function at its natural resonance. Taking time to breathe will allow the voice to be its expressive best.

Increase your vocabulary: write down every word you come across you are not sure of. Use the dictionary and thesaurus to help you find even more expressive ways to communicate.

Remember the Punch Line: think of how the joke ends, have a good exit line, and know when to get out of Dodge!

The Young one, at the "Playhouse in the Park"
Cincinnati, Ohio, 1961

CHAPTER 2

"Foolish Fisticuffs"

The manly art of self-defense in today's society is outmoded, outdated, and not much of a defense at all in these difficult times. In fact people blow each other away every day for just looking cross-eyed at each other.

With children under eleven and twelve carrying guns and using them, older guys beating people senseless or worse for the slightest provocation, it's tough out there.

So tough, in fact, that the fine art of using your mouth instead of your muscle can mean more than success: it can mean basic survival.

Of course I am not saying that even a gift of gab can extricate you from every situation or confrontation. But fists are useless when you are out numbered and unarmed.

Only Superman can outrun a bullet. So, at times, talking may be your only option. In fact, these life-threatening altercations aside, your ability to handle your mouth can prove a far more effective defense and prove far less wearing on body and soul.

Once again you have to be sure you are not only listening to the other person, but you are understanding what they are about as well. "Easy for you to say," you think.

Arguments between friends and loved ones usually stem from wanting to be in control, or needing to be right. Most of it boils down to ego or lack thereof.

Once you are willing to admit you are not perfect, not always the smartest, and not always right, you can be less emotionally controlled by the situation.

From that point on you are in the driver's seat. You will be the one who makes the decision as to where the conversation is headed, what road it will take, and what will be the ultimate conclusion, or destination.

That kind of personal control is hard to achieve when you are screaming at the top of your lungs. So relax, take a deep breath and calm yourself. Now, state your point, and really communicate.

When you are recording your friendly conversations between consenting confidants or intimates, I advise you to

Really listen to each other.

Actually by the very process of recording, unless you forgot that you were taping, the dialogue between you both was controlled, at least subconsciously, by knowing the machine was on.

Your voice probably stayed at a lower pitch, and you took a little more time to express yourself more definitively than with-out the recorder on.

There is something about the recording process that intimidates people. It's the sense of permanence, much akin to your words being etched in stone, that makes you think before you speak. Nobody wants to be seen as a fool in the eyes of their peers.

If only we could keep that uppermost in our mind in every-day heated discussions or confrontations with the people in our lives. Everybody starts to get hot under the collar once in awhile.

But it doesn't have to be that way. Just take a minute, smile and relax.

You have read my book and they haven't.

You are now thinking and speaking with precision and effectiveness while they're not. You have been able, with practice and discipline, to separate yourself from purely ego- and emotionally- based rhetoric, using logic to prove your point, and they're screaming at the top of their lungs about being right.

You are speaking in a mellow modulated pitch close to your natural resonance sounding like a winner, and they are frothing at the mouth. They have not only lost the argument, but odds are, their voice as well.

OK, I agree that's the perfect scenario, but you see my point. Use your mouth instead of your muscle. Those who talk and walk away, live to win (and talk) another day.

**Control your mouth and you
can win everyday!**

Certainly drugs and guns have made our society a battle ground where getting through the day without a major war is more than survival, it is a miracle.

You can't reason with someone who is out of their mind on drugs or drink. They have lost the ability to think like a rational human being, and cannot be dealt with using logic or facts.

You can sometimes use the insanity of the situation as an advantage to extricate yourself from what appears to be a "no-win" situation.

A few years ago I was a member of a theatrical workshop in Van Nuys, California. We would put on plays and musicals for the community, not charging admission, and use our performances and reviews to get ourselves paying professional work in television and films.

This particular afternoon I was in the theatre alone cleaning the bathrooms and vacuuming the lobby, as we "volunteers" do, to keep the place presentable.

Suddenly, the front door is slammed open, and this guy stumbles in from the street. I'm no runt, standing 6'6" and weighing in at about 235#, but this guy was big!

Big arms, big chest, big fists, BIG!

He looked strong, mean and a little crazy. In fact he was looking for trouble and wasn't going to leave the building until he found it.

I didn't want him to do damage to the premises or to me personally, but he was spoiling for a fight.

I had that feeling, deep in the pit of my stomach, that if I got into a fight I was sure to get badly hurt.

I couldn't leave him alone in the building, so I decided to talk. I would talk **"AS IF"** I was crazier than he was. Sure I had done many roles on television where I had played a character that was written as crazy or stupid, but here was a case where I had to convince this guy I was more out of my mind than he was.

I wasn't sure what he really wanted, but I knew it included pain and suffering, so I kept playing crazy. In a few minutes I could see he started to think I was as capable of as much random violence and anger as he was.

I guess he figured it was not worth the effort to continue the confrontation, because he finally left with my relentless ranting and raving in his ears.

Under the visual picture of this scene you would probably see the disclaimer "Do not try this at home. Feat accomplished by a trained professional."

Even in this bizarre situation a gift of gab, and a little playing **"AS IF,"** save my bacon by giving me an "out" with an unarmed maniac.

Note: never mouth off to a guy with a gun!

Often being very specific about what you want to say really helps you get your point across. Subtle inferences and obscure illustrations just won't get the job done.

In order to be a vocal success, train yourself to speak to the point, don't beat around the bush, and always say what you mean.

It seems few people today are willing to speak their mind. In my opinion, we have become a nation of followers, cattle herded from one (pen), place, to another.

We should demand and expect to be given the common courtesies and service we pay for.

That is the **"Bitch,"** part of the title of this book, and we will deal extensively with your rights, and how to get them, in subsequent chapters.

Back to getting your point across. I was shooting a "movie of the week" for television entitled "Target Risk." It was a ridiculous part. I was the bad guy, the enforcer: four times I have a confrontation with the leading man, and four times in a row he beats the crap out of me.

Now that's stupid, but not as dopey as the "star" of the film who tore up my leg, for real, in one of the movie's first fight scenes.

We were setting up this camera shot in the middle of the fight. He was supposed to make it look like he flips me over his shoulder and onto the concrete sidewalk.

Rather than stopping just before the flip, so that they could put some pads down on the concrete, and reset the camera, he continued with the stunt. The camera missed the shot, and I hit the sidewalk full force, tearing up my wardrobe and my leg, with blood everywhere.

We had to suspend shooting to clean up the mess, and sew up my leg. When I asked why in the hell he didn't stop the flip, he replied "I just felt it, and went with the moment."

Getting to the point about getting your point across: a few days later we had another fight scene where the star once again beats the stuffing out of me.

This time I made it abundantly clear to the director on the set that if I went down again, the star was going with me. There was no way I was going to be unnecessarily hurt a second time. His face was going into the ground if he

"Just went with the moment," and this time he would "feel it" for sure!

Well, my talk to the person in charge did the trick, because when he arrived on the set, everyone followed the fight choreography, the scene went smoothly, and I was treated well for the rest of the shoot.

To make things happen you have to talk to the right people. When things go wrong it is no use complaining to your buddy or your friends. You have to get the word to those who can make a difference, not those who will just agree with you and nod sympathetically.

Decide, from now on, you are going to take the time and effort to get to the person or persons who can effect change.

Get to the decision makers

That probably means going up the chain of command. At first it can be intimidating, but you must tough it out if you want to alter things for the better.

In the last chapter I said it's not always what you say, it's how you say it. The lesson to be learned in this chapter is, it is not only how you say it, but whom you say it to.

Before you can **"Bitch, Pitch and get Rich,"** you have to find the right person to **"Bitch"** to. That "right" person varies with every problem and every situation.

You probably already know the appropriate person to **"Bitch"** to. You just don't know how to start, what is the right time, or if you can do it.

Many people are a little afraid, or shy, or intimidated. They worry they will exacerbate the situation, or just plain stick their foot in it.

If you feel a little like this, the next chapter has some suggestions that will help you overcome these problems.

CHAPTER REVIEW

Really listen to each **other:** be sure you not only hear the other person, but try to understand what they are about as well. Sense how they feel, and what you hear.

Use your mouth instead of muscle: those who talk and walk away, live to win another day. Keep the mouth in control and at the ready.

Get to the "Decision Maker": if you want to effect change you have to get to the level where policy can be made. Don't waste your time complaining to friends and sycophants (look it up?).

Bitch to the right person: the lesson to be learned in this chapter is it is not only how you say it, but whom you say it to.

And lest we forget, with all the nuts out there, no matter how confident you are in your linguistic skills,

Never mouth off to a guy with a gun!

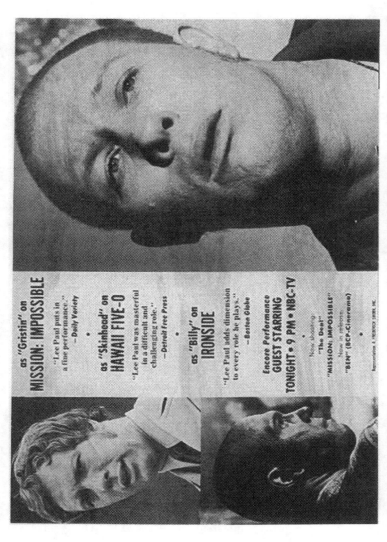

as "Gristin" on
MISSION: IMPOSSIBLE

"Lee Paul puts in
a fine performance."
—*Daily Variety*

as "Skinhead" on
HAWAII FIVE-O

"Lee Paul was masterful
in a difficult and
challenging role."
—*Detroit Free Press*

as "Billy" on
IRONSIDE

"Lee Paul adds dimension
to every role he plays."
—*Boston Globe*

Encore Performance
GUEST STARRING
TONIGHT • 9 PM • NBC-TV

Now showing
"The Deal"
"MISSION: IMPOSSIBLE"

Now in release:
"SIN" (BCP-Cinerama)

Daily Variety (Entertainment Paper) ad listing 5 TV roles in Hollywood, CA, 1971

CHAPTER 3

Imagination and the Magic "AS IF"

I'm sure that growing up in New York and needing to talk my way out of numerous situations throughout my formative years, helped develop my "gift of gab."

In order to be heard above the din of the city, I learned to talk loud, fast and often. Of course in those days I wasn't concerned with how my voice sounded, or how precisely I expressed myself.

When I talked with a friend about starting this "self-help" book, he said be sure to include a chapter for those people who, like himself, had difficulty speaking up, or making themselves heard when they had something important to say.

This was the genesis for many of the topics in

"Bitch, Pitch and get Rich."

Some individuals are basically shy, or afraid to be put in the spotlight. Even though they feel very strongly about a point they would like to make or a position they want to defend, they find real difficulty in being heard and heeded.

Now, you don't have to grow up in Brooklyn, be an actor or an even an extrovert, to be a "mouth" and use it.

In fact, I am often surprised how inarticulate some of our well-known stars and entertainers are, when it comes to talking extemporaneously, especially as themselves.

With a script they are brilliant, but ask them to talk off the cuff, even on topics close to them and they stumble like the rest of us.

So that means all of us can, with work, practice and diligence, develop an effective gift of gab.

Work with the fundamentals discussed in the previous chapters daily until they become second nature, and you will improve.

1. **Start reading out loud:** This not only improves your reading and comprehension, but it starts to

familiarize you with the sound of your own voice as others hear you.

2. **Work on your memory:** Carry a note pad or voice recorder so that when you think of something you want to remember you have it.

3. **Develop your personal pitch:** By finding the natural resonance in your voice you will allow your voice to be its most expressive and effective.

4. **Record your personal conversations:** In the playback you hear if you make sense and sound believable. You will become conscious of the pauses and flubs we all make at the start.

5. **Look up words and spellings:** The dictionary and thesaurus are the development tools to better verbal understanding, in-creased vocabulary, and more expressive communication.

All of these steps you can work on in the privacy of your room or home. You can make mistakes, sound foolish, or get just tongue- tied and no one will know but you.

Fifteen minutes a day with the voice recorder, and standing in front of the mirror as you talk "<u>out loud</u>," will help you gain the verbal skill and confidence you need to be your personal best, and win the war of words.

In fact, the simple act of talking aloud, at a higher vocal level than you use in normal conversation, will do wonders in bringing you out of your shell.

Once you start to get comfortable with how you sound out loud, and become excited by your increased ability to express yourself, talking to strangers or superiors will be easier and a lot less nerve racking.

All of this will not happen overnight. But knowing that your very success and survival in the competitive world outside depends on the effective use of your mouth, you will, with progress, quickly concur it's worth your time and effort.

Talk out loud, in front of a mirror, and record it!

As you see gradual, but steady, improvement in your verbal skills you will want to test your new linguistic prowess on the battle field of the world around you.

Knowing how to talk is very important, but understanding how people think is also a necessary skill needed to win in the tournament of life.

I am not going to advocate you enroll in a psychology course or attend lectures on human motivation (though they have their place and merit). I am going to suggest that simple observation of the people we come in daily contact with can be of great value in our battle to win the war of words.

When I came to Hollywood in the mid 60's one of my first acting teachers was the renowned Jeff Corey. Young and just beginning my career, I remember being surprised at how many of the people in the class had no intention of becoming actors or performers.

There were doctors, lawyers, and many people from the business world. I wondered why "civilians" such as these, were taking acting lessons, until I began to understand what Mr. Corey was teaching.

It was not so much how to "act," but how to honestly "react" to people and situations around us. He taught us how to observe human behavior by simply watching and remembering how people looked and what people did in everyday life.

Observation is a major tool in beginning to understand human behavior and feelings. Without a masters degree in body language, we know by watching someone closely if they are angry, happy, anxious or sad, etc., just by looking.

It takes a bit of courage to watch someone closely, if we think they know we are looking. Observing the physical attitude of a person, can tell you a great deal about how they feel and some times even what they are thinking.

Where do you think the phrase "poker face" comes from? Of course an expert poker player knows to look at more than just faces to get clues about his opponents' thoughts and cards.

So many of Jeff Corey's students were there to study life. What motivates people, what are the basic emotions, and how they are universally expressed? What is common to the human spirit? How does physicality and our closeness to people and things that matter to us affect us all?

It seems almost a maxim that people who are withdrawn or shy are also reluctant to get physically close to anyone beyond the smallest circle of intimates.

In today's society there seems to be unwritten rule: "Don't touch," And I don't even mean in a sexual way. Just don't get close to people and don't let them get close to you.

Besides being shy, people who sense this, are fearful of infringing another person's space, and therefore remain distant and uninvolved.

The trick in living life fully is getting involved!

Getting involved is a major stimulus to expressing yourself and beginning to break out of your shell. You may have strong convictions. You may have a deep-seated need to express your opinion. You may want to offer suggestions for constructive change.

Forget that it's a little scary sometimes getting started and *Do It!*

Through dialogue and personal contact you will find new avenues for expression. Sharing your ideas and opinions with others begins the process by which you will develop the confidence to talk one on one, with anyone, about all the things that are important to you.

This is how you develop and grow as an individual. Your personal involvement and the enriching experience of sharing your ideas with others makes life stimulating and rewarding.

You have to Stand Up and be Counted

Lee Paul

A few years ago I was teaching an extension course entitled "Acting for non-actors"at one of those adult evening universities.

I'm sure the idea found its genesis in those early classes with Mr. Corey. Most of the students in the class were there to learn how to break into acting. The school had listed a number of my television and movie credits in their brochure.

A number however were professionals who had specific problems with speaking in public or in the scope of their job.

One particular woman was an attorney, who though skilled in preparing briefs, became nervous, flustered and unable to talk when she stood up in court to present her case.

Mark how vital your verbal skills can be

With all her preparation and expertise, she couldn't get her point across successfully in the courtroom. Outside the courtroom, in my classroom, she was able to talk about her difficulty, so, with support from the class and some strong direction, we helped her find a path to overcome her fear and frustration of speaking in public.

It is a fact that many of the tools we develop as actors are of immeasurable use to people

34

who never set foot on a stage or in front of a camera.

These new skills we have been working on will benefit us immensely, whatever field or endeavor we pursue.

Which brings us back to the many aspects that makes us who we are-- the varied facets that make up **YOU!**

We all have more than one side to our personality. Certainly we can use our imagination to talk **"AS IF"** we were the warrior, **"AS IF"** we were the critic, **"AS IF"** we were the observer...

We can do this because what we really are, as people, is the sum of all those identities and parts we play in life.

Without attempting to be a psychologist, I believe when someone says they are shy, perhaps it is their inner critic not allowing them to express themselves.

The "critic" in them says, "Don't stick your neck out," or "Don't look like a fool," or "You can't afford to make a mistake."

The good news is that we can just as easily listen to the inner voice of the **warrior**, and instead we will be saying, "I can handle this confrontation," or "I can make my point," or "I can win this battle of words."

Thinking and talking **"AS IF"** we were in command quite often will put us in command. At the very least it will earn us the respect of being a leader, and give us the forum to express our views and perhaps persuade others toward our point of view.

So what am I saying?

If you really want to learn to use your mouth effectively, *you can.* If you want to take command and make decisions, *you can*, however you feel about yourself at this very moment. You can change for the better. You can always improve and grow as an individual.

Shy, withdrawn, nervous? You can talk **"AS IF"** you were the dynamic and persuasive person you want to be, and you will be.

Start slowly. Next time you get in a con- versation and feel you are unable to get your point across, just start talking **"AS IF"** you are winning the verbal battle.

Before you know it the tide will turn and you will be holding your own. In time you will begin to win the war of words, have that "gift of gab," and be on the way to a "master mouth."

Have the right attitude!

Attitude is important in getting your point across, but it is not the complete answer. Remember that knowledge and the correct facts are the bullets of truth with which you will shoot down the argument of your verbal opponent.

Prepare yourself by reading the dictionary for proper word usage, the thesaurus for increased vocabulary, and all the books you can on the subjects you want to discuss and debate.

Even with all the training and expertise at your command, you will sometimes be defeated. No one wins every battle, verbal or otherwise.

The only way to keep your verbal tactics sharp and at the ready is practice. It's your job to see that you are prepared and proficient enough to be sure you ultimately win the war.

Practice sharpens verbal tactics

Once a week, on average, for the last 20 years I have gotten together with two good friends to have dinner and engage in some verbal jousting. After each dinner, we discuss current events, the arts, ancient history, whatever topic is of primary interest at that moment. And we get into some pretty heated discussions.

It is a tribute to our enduring friendships that we have maintained our civility and contact all these years, for we have gotten into some real battles.

I'm sure the fact that we have always had an encyclopedia, dictionary and thesaurus, or our new lap top, at the ready, has helped keep us friends.

Regardless of our opinions, we have always checked the facts. Through the years it's been a terrific ongoing exercise in increasing our knowledge, and expanding our ability to express our individual points of view. Not to mention the fun of being right on the money.

Those weekly sojourns have increased our knowledge, expanded our ability to express our individual points of view and stimulated the little gray cells.

Have you been looking up every word you don't recognize, or fully understand?

Instead of going out or watching television, why don't you meet once a week with some close friends or family and participate in some verbal jousting?

Start by discussing some subject you are all familiar with. Record the dialogue (again with mutual consent).

Listen and decide who sounds believable and who, by checking the facts, is telling the truth. You will find it's not always the same person-- or yourself.

As time goes on you can introduce new subjects. Here is where your i-Pad will keep the discussion out of the realm of opinion and ego, and in the real world of facts.

As an aside, this mutual agreement to record the dialog between your friends can sorely test those friendships, so pick them carefully.

CHAPTER REVIEW

Observation: is the major tool in beginning to understand human behavior. Develop the courage to really look at people, and besides learning a great deal about how they really feel, you'll greatly improve your ability to communicate verbally with them.

Get Involved: is the primary stimulus to expressing yourself. Sharing your ideas and opinions with others begins the way by which you develop the confidence to talk one-to-one, with anyone

Talk "AS IF": there are many sides to our personalities. Each of us has many facets to draw from when expressing ourselves. Use that part of your personality that can most effectively handle the situation and you will be more effective and successful.

Stand up and be counted: Once you begin to feel confident about expressing yourself, speak up. Let yourself be heard. Take the plunge and start talking. Make your point with assurance and authority and before long you will not only be stating your position, but making your point as well. **DO IT!**

Notes and Observations

....

....

....

....

....

....

....

....

....

....

....

....

....

....

....

....

....

Backstage at the Sands, La Vegas, NV
with the legendary Sammy David Jr., 1968

CHAPTER 4

"Testing the Tributaries"

O.K., you have worked on your voice, read voraciously on subjects of interest to you, started to increase your vocabulary by looking up every word you are unfamiliar with, and even done verbal battle with your friends.

You are ready to defend the truth, fight for justice, and uphold the way of western civilization.

Using your newfound mouth, you are going to get the recognition you deserve and the service you demand. With the verbal adroitness you now have at your command, you are now determined to excel, succeed, and prosper!

Great! just be sure you remember what you say is as important as when you say it!

The correct facts, the undeniable truth, and the power of your persuasive position, don't mean a hill of beans if you pop off at the wrong time. Opening your mouth is one thing, putting your foot in it is another.

Even if you feel you are witty, charming, and fabulously funny, you still have to carefully choose the time and the place to talk. We all make mistakes when it comes to using our mouth.

One of my worse "foot in mouth moments" was on the set of "McMillan and Wife", the television series that starred Rock Hudson and Susan St. James.

You already know how tall I am and Mr. Hudson was almost my height. This was not the first time we had met, and I mentioned it when we were introduced the first day I was on the show, hoping to establish a friendly rapport.

In television and films, when they are lighting a scene before the actual filming, they often use stand-ins to take the place of the principle performers. That way they can get the lighting right and the actors can study their lines, prepare their part, or just get away from the hot lights, until they are ready to roll the camera.

44

Since none of the official stand-ins were tall enough I said, "Rock, would you mind standing in for me while they light my close-up, everyone is so short?"

Talk about a Foot in Mouth moment! I told you everyone can make a mistake!

He didn't laugh, he didn't smile, he didn't say a word. In fact the entire set became as quiet as a tomb (mine). He just kept staring at me.

The next few minutes seemed like hours. With that numbing panic that you feel when you know your career is on the line, all I could taste was foot.

The twenty odd years that had passed since we first met back in Marietta College, Ohio, for the World Premier of his "Battle Hymn" flashed by me as before death, and even if I didn't die, I felt my acting career was dead already.

Thankfully "Mr. Hudson" finally smiled, started to laugh and let me off the hook! I took the first breath in what seemed an hour, and the set came back to life as well.

This little episode illustrates the fine line between being smart and being a "smart ass," and you must learn where that movable line is.

I say the SAL (smart ass line) is movable because it changes according to the situation. You can, with skill and experience, expand the envelope of your mouth's acceptability.

In some spots you can get away with a lot more than in others. Even with the skills, a good part of talking effectively is sizing up the situation.

When you walk into a room and/or enter into a conversation the first thing you must tune into is the **"Power."** Every situation has somebody in charge.

At any one given moment someone has the focus, is in charge, and has the **"Power."**

And it is not always the same person. Often in the course of the conversation the positions change. You have to:

"Pick out the Power"

Talking to the wrong person, even when you are right on the money, is a waste of your time!

LOOK AND LISTEN!

Of course in friendly repartee it might not matter as much, but in a business context it can mean a lot more than getting your point across. It can mean your job.

Like it or not in the workaday world we are controlled and confined by the hierarchy of the system. That is why, if we are to advance the truths (troops) and win the battle, we must have a clear objective.

We must get to the "Decision Maker"

In every group, in every discussion, there are those who make the final decision. Eventually, that person may be you. Until that time, to get your point across, to effect real change, to win a battle of words that counts, you must find and challenge the

"Decision Maker"

When my wife has a problem with the car, she starts to list off all the things that are going wrong. I always say, "Don't tell me, I'm not the mechanic."

Learn to "Bitch" to the right person.

Unless you want to tell your story over and over and over, you must try to get to the person who can effect change from the start. Obviously the mechanic will be the one to repair the car.

How many times have you gotten on the phone with a problem and found every time you were transferred you had to start your story all over again?

Of course it's not always easy finding the **"Decision Maker."** It seems a lot of the time they are unavailable, or busy deciding something else.

But by and large, I have found the higher you go up the corporate ladder to solve a problem the tougher it becomes. The reward comes from finding the right person in management with the authority and concern to effect change.

But remember, it is not enough to **"Bitch"** about a problem, you must try to come up with a solution to that problem if you can.

Don't just complain, think of a solution!

Try to **"Pitch"** an idea for effective change as well. That is the only way the system will improve. Even if the decision makers don't have an answer at that time, you can at least make them think about one.

You have to jump in and get your feet wet!

    A. Stick your neck out
    B. Take a chance
    C. Get involved
    D. STAND UP AND BE COUNTED

And that's what you have to do. Regardless of what you are doing now, if you are unhappy or unfulfilled, you can change. Dig into your innermost feelings and you will discover what is truly important to you.

If you have a dream, go for it. If you don't have a dream, find a new goal. Start using your mind and your mouth to reach it. With work and caring you can make your dream a reality.

A friend of mine has wanted to be a singer all his life. He has a fine voice and a good gift of gab, but he has never made the total commitment. He has always found a reason for putting it off. And you know what? He is running out of time.

Life is too short for excuses

Get your feet wet by "Testing the Tributaries." Even if you are happy in your work, there is always room for improvement. Start challenging yourself and those around you by using your mouth to improve the situation, find solutions and effect change.

And it is not all work-- it can be fun. There is nothing like proving a point, finding a solution, or even getting a laugh, to make you feel good about yourself.

All that philosophy aside, life in general can be a hell of a lot more enjoyable when you don't feel pushed around, taken advantage of, or simply ignored.

Opening your mouth at the right time, and to the right person, will get you the rewards of life you so richly deserve.

CHAPTER REVIEW

Look and Listen: In every conversation, in every room, someone has the focus, someone is in charge. Find that person.

Pick out the Power: Talking to the wrong person, even when you are right, is a waste of time. Get to the **"Decision Maker."**

Don't just Complain: Try to think of a solution. If anyone is going to improve the system, it's got to be you. **"Pitch"** a new idea.

Start to assert yourself: We are not cattle to be herded around, led by our noses to whatever pen or point they decide.

Jump in and get your feet wet: It's the easiest way to get involved. Nothing happens on the sidelines except waiting for something to happen. You have to get into the game of life.

Stand up and be counted: Stick your neck out, and take a chance. You'll lose a few verbal battles, but you'll get better and stronger, and with the increased confidence that comes with being in the fray, you will begin to win.

Life is too short for excuses: Don't waste it on reasons why you not involved.

Working in automotive sales at Vista Lincoln
Mercury, Woodland Hills, CA, 2008

CHAPTER 5

"Battling the Behemoths"

The only difference between the "Big Boys" and the little store on the corner, when it comes to people out there in Television Land, the consumer, us-- is accessibility.

Do they have an 800 line or don't they?

With the shop on the corner you can walk up to the owner, the **"Decision Maker,"** "Bitch," and more likely than not, have your problem taken care of. Adhering to the time honored tradition that the customer is always right, especially when he or she is in your face, the **"Decision Maker"** might even listen to a suggestion. That is, if you **"Pitch"** one or two.

With the "Big Boys," chances are their corporate headquarters are not in your home town, and even if they were, you have to get past the guard. That leaves the telephone, the fax, or e-mail.

You would be surprised at the number of multinational companies that don't have 800 toll free lines for their customers.

And if you check out the internet and go to a "Big" company's home page, you can spend hours trying to get any phone numbers at all.

Still there are companies, large and small, that list with 1-800 directory services. Of course it's all automated now with nobody live on the other end. You cope.

For a person who lives by his mouth, the best thing in the world, next to an ear, is a mouthpiece. A few pages back I suggested you get your feet wet and start testing your mouth on the telephone.

What better place to start using your emerging gift of gab. That's where you can really start to **"Bitch and Pitch,"** and the worst thing that can happen to you, if you are not making your point, or they're just rude, is that they hang up!

Already I can hear you saying, I'm not a "Pitchman." Maybe you're not a "Salesman." But think about it, whatever your vocation, you are. If you are not selling a product or a service, you are selling yourself, or at least your ideas.

Salesman is not a dirty word!

When you **"Bitch"** about a problem and **"Pitch"** a suggestion or solution, you are selling yourself and your opinion. So say it, you are a "salesman," and what better product could there be than **you**?

Of course the millions of salesman out there that earn a very respectable living in sales, already know how relevant the **"you"** factor is.

No product or service, regardless of how great, will ever be sold with out the man or woman selling it, knowing and believing they are as good as what they are selling.

"You" the salesman, the pitchman, must know, accept, and acknowledge your own personal worth.

Once you decide you are valuable and important:

Once you realize you are worth attention and respect;

Once you start to demand the quality and service you are entitled to;

Once you see that as an individual, you are as important as any company;

Once you believe that an idea, spoken or written, is mightier than the sword;

You are ready to "Battle the Behemoths"

Some times it is hard to remember that a company or organization, no matter how large, is made up of individuals. Strange, because often our opinion of that company as a whole depends upon our interaction with only one or two people in it.

But whether we decide we want to do business with a company or not, we still deal with that **megalith** one person at a time. And we now know we can do that! All it often takes is

"Time and Tenacity"

and that elusive "800 line," to get to the

"Decision Maker"

One of my pet peeves is the lack of service in this great country-- **service**, and getting the quality you pay for, which I will cover in slightly fanatical detail in pages to come.

The idea of service has become so foreign to this country, that even "foreign" companies that do business here, feel they can get away without it.

We, the consumers, are partly to blame. One of the main goals of this book is to get everyone to use their mouths, to demand better service and greater quality.

For me, the 800 service line, or lack of one, somehow symbolizes the collapse of service in this country. How many times have you found there is a toll free 800 line for orders with a company, but if you want service or just help with instructions, it's on your dime?

At the beginning of this chapter, I mentioned the difference between getting to the right person in one of these corporate behemoths and in the mom and pop store.

Remember I said not only do you have to **"Bitch,"** but you have to **"Bitch"** to the right person. You have to try to get to the individual who can effect permanent change, or at the very least, solve your immediate problem.

Personally I want to do that at their expense. If I am going to take the time, I feel they should be paying for the call.

**And herein lies the great
800 line run-around**

When I first wrote this book, I used an early word processor (before personal computers and lap-tops). It was made by Panasonic. Their American corporate headquarters is in Secaucus, New Jersey. They had 4 Regional Administration Centers, with service stations in 16 states. They include a toll free number in the instructions.

Sounds pretty good so far, right? Wrong!

First, the toll free line was not at Panasonic, it is a referral service, a division of Panasonic, that gives you your closest repair center according to zip codes.

These <u>repair</u> services knows nothing about the products, or their operation, so they cannot answer questions about how a particular machine works or answer any questions you might have.

At this point I don't need a repair man. I have operational questions and need answers.

A particular problem had developed with the word processing program in my machine, but it was not broken.

Living on the West Coast, I am not about to call New Jersey on my dime... at least, not yet.

Next I try a local Panasonic dealer, who informs me they only handle office products, like answering machines, faxes, telephones... but no word processors. So, even though I don't need a repairman at this time, I call a repair center.

I'm in luck: one of the 16 nationwide repair centers is in my local dialing area. However, their line is always busy, and when it does finally connect, I get an answering machine saying leave a message and they will get back to me. They never do.

I decide to go to the national mail order house I bought the unit from. They are in St. Cloud, Minnesota, and have a toll free line for ordering, but not for customer service. The machine is still giving me a problem, and I am determined to get an answer.

So it's on to 800 information, where I am informed that there is no 800 number for my area to Panasonic in New Jersey. When I ask from what area there is a toll free line, I am informed they are not allowed to give me that information.

What's a mouth to do? I can't get to anyone, let alone a **"Decision Maker"** regarding my question or complaint. I still refuse to pay for a call to New Jersey.

After explaining to a supervisor (by this time they transferred me because I didn't fit the pattern) she finally gives me the long sought after Panasonic 800 line.

I'm happy as a clam at high tide, until I call and realize it's the same repair referral number I got with my instructions. Foiled again!

O.K., I won't call New Jersey, but I will call the Regional Center in Cypress California. It's just a few area codes away. I call collect and I am informed, as when I called Secaucus, they do not accept collect calls.

Undaunted I call again (still on their dime) and when they pick up I say I can't hear them. "Can you hear me?" I ask.

They say they can hear me fine, and I say, "Would you mind calling me back, there must be a bad connection on my end." Lo and behold they do.

It's a good thing it's on their dime because it takes me twenty minutes of transferring before I get to someone who "can't" answer my question, but does finally give me the secret toll free line to their main office in New Jersey.

As a final irony, Panasonic transfers me back to California, to the same repair center with the answering machine. This time, perhaps because the call is coming in on a hot line from Jersey, they pick up the phone. I am informed they don't repair word processors there, but one of the technicians has one and answers my question. SUCCESS!

That's what I mean about **"Time and Tenacity,"** and that's what I mean about the lack of service commitment on the part of these big companies.

I love the challenge of putting things right, and by the end of this book I hope you will too. When I buy something I want it to work in its entirety, as it was designed to function. I don't want to live with even a small problem.

You will find that once you start demanding the service and quality you pay for, not only will you feel a sense of pride in yourself, you will develop a new sense of appreciation of the intrinsic value of everything around you.

Using **"Time and Tenacity"** to plow through Panasonic, I learned a great deal about my word processor and what it can and cannot do. I appreciate, even more fully, the capabilities of the machine because I have learned almost all I could about it.

Along the way I continued to increase my ability to use my mouth-- to get answers, to correct problems, and with a few choice words to Secaucus, New Jersey, maybe even improve the system. I **"Bitch"**ed, and then I **Pitch"**ed.

Knowledge feeds our mind and enriches our appreciation and enjoyment of life around us. Wisdom is wealth and power. Far more than just financial, I believe that is what getting **"Rich"** is all about.

The higher you go up the corporate level in your unending quest for the **"Decision Maker,"** the tougher the climb becomes. But to effect change, right a wrong, or get the job done, you have to develop the strength and skill of your mouth.

The problems and challenges start at the bottom. In almost every business environment, at the lower levels, people are given the responsibility, but not the authority, to do their job. So you have to work at reaching the people who have the answers or who can effect change. But the rewards are great for those who get it done.

CHAPTER REVIEW

Salesmanship is not a dirty word: If you are not selling a product or service, you are selling yourself, or your ideas.

Use those 800 lines: And not just for ordering, but for information and complaints. If a company doesn't offer free customer service lines, tell them you'll be doing business with those that do.

Bitch, but to the right person: Unless you want to tell your story over and over with no results, get to a **"Decision Maker,"** the person who can effect change.

Use your mouth, and speak your mind: Only by being heard will you get your point across, stimulate solutions for improvement, and reap the rewards of quality and service you so richly deserve.

The cold of the ice & snow at Glacier Bay
Alaska via the Carnival Spirit, circa 2006

CHAPTER 6

The Overseas Connotation

When I first listed this chapter in the proposed index, I called it "The Overseas Connection," but as I began to fill in the blanks, I realized "connection" was not an adequate word for the whole story.

This is where the Thesaurus is invaluable.

As you proceed you will notice an inexorable nexus (time to get out that dictionary) between the use of one's mouth and the use of one's pen.

Needing a challenge, I thought you might not be sure of the meaning of the word, "inexorable," but I was pretty sure you would have to look up the word "nexus." (I did) Only when I was looking for a more apt word than "connection" did I find it in the thesaurus.

Believe me, there is great fun and value in finding new words to more accurately define your thoughts. The more precisely you express yourself, the more clearly and forcefully you will be able to get your point across. And that holds true for writing as well.

Consulting the good books, I decided on "connotation." In Webster's New World Dictionary, circa 1956, from my college days at Marietta, Ohio, the third definition seemed the most apropos.

If you are going to increase your vocabulary, and learn new and more accurate ways of expressing your thoughts and ideas, you have to keep the books at the ready and use them.

Dictionary, Thesaurus, Famous Quotes

In fact, another of my writer friends suggested I include an appropriate quote from a famous person in history at the beginning or end of each chapter.

I haven't done that, but at this moment the quote by Philip Dormer Stanhope (4th Earl of Chesterfield)-- "Advice is seldom welcome; and those who want it the most always like it the least.," seems painfully to the point.

Luckily many of the verbal skills we have been working on translate to paper remarkably well:

in fact, now that you are getting used to being heard and headed, it is a remarkably easy transition to the written word.

In the celerity (dictionary?) of living in this country, Americans have had little time for the finer points of the art of the communique. Some of the common courtesies familiar to most of the civilized world seem sadly deficient in the states.

Part of the difficulty in reaching the **"Decision Maker"** at home or abroad, is getting them to pick up the phone, let alone return a call. That time-honored phrase, "Who may I say is calling?," more often than not is a prelude to, "I'm sorry, they're not in, would you care to leave your name and number?" If you are that lucky!

That's where **"Time and Tenacity"** again are so important. Keep talking and keep dialing. It's worth it.

When dealing with people overseas, however it's a whole different ball game. Whether it's because of the pace or the people, they answer calls (when the phone works) and return correspondence.

Since I'm not in the habit of calling Europe to resolve a problem, I write. In fact, as an actor,

I have written people in my profession all over the world.

It has been a constant source of amazement to me that I will receive a ready reply from London, England, when I won't get even a postcard from Studio City, here in Los Angeles.

But back to talking, since this book is all about

"Success at the tip of your tongue"

and the ways to ensure effective and compelling speech.

One of the most interesting aspects of our speaking voice is that it sounds very much the same, even as we grow older. It's going to be with you all your life. So keep working on the exercises to make your voice as expressive and commanding as possible.

The ageless voice

Often when I meet a person after talking to them on the phone, I find them to be physically a older than the sound of their voice. Vocally we seem to stay forever young.

It's your voice for a lifetime. Why not learn to make it as expressive and compelling as possible?

Everything you do is a learning process. This is especially true if you have an insatiable curiosity about things, as I do.

Besides that, learning about yourself and the every day world you come in contact with, can be extremely interesting and rewarding.

Talking about continuity and a commitment to service that the overseas companies seem to excel in, this next story truly illustrates the point. It also underscores the reason for taking the time to allow your natural curiosity to lead you down a new path of discovery and enrichment.

A few years ago I was in this little antique shop in Canoga Park, California. Browsing around, I spied these two metal combs. They were tarnished and a bit worn, but looked interesting. A little polish would do wonders, so I bought them.

To some that would be the end of the story; to me it was just the beginning. How old were they? What were they used for? Where were they made?

The proprietor shook her head, smiled, and said she didn't know, but since I was so interested she would give me a break on the price.

After a few more questions and some polite negotiations she had my $8 and I had her 2 combs. By using my mouth I was a few dollars richer, but the best was yet to come.

The only clue was the stamping on the combs. On one side it said, "Spratt's Patent Ltd. Sole Agents, London." And on the reverse side it said, "Binns Specilities, Reg. #109171."

The smaller of the two had an "S," and the larger a "4." This piqued my curiosity, and wanting more information, I decided to write. Not having an address, but knowing the sense of tradition the English pride themselves on, I thought I'd take a chance.

Sending only a postcard describing the combs, I addressed it to Spratt's Patent Ltd., London, England, and popped it in the post, as the British would say. Not even a zip code.

About a month later I received a letter from one Dr. A.D. Walker, Retired. The letterhead said, Spillers Foods, Paddock Office, Moulton Road, Kentford, Nr. Newmarket, Suffolk, CB8 8QU, England. How's that for an address?

It seems that Spillers Foods had taken over Spratt's Patent Ltd., and the good doctor was on a retainer to handle all current correspondence to the old company. Fifty years later he was still at it. I found out all about the combs, the company, and five decades of English marketing history.

All for eight dollars, a little of my time and allowing my curiosity to work its enriching magic.

Learn about life and all its wonders

Those little combs have started more conversations, and a gift of gab, fueled by the facts, ferreted out by my curiosity about its past, has resulted in meeting new people, establishing fresh business contacts, and yes, even culminated in money-making deals.

It's amazing what a little gift of gab can do

Enlarging your vocabulary, increasing the activity of your little gray cells, and effectively using your mouth, will help you to get ahead, increase your income, and change your life for the better.

By maximizing your potential as person, you will reach your goals, fulfill your dreams, and with dedication and perseverance, fulfill your destiny!

CHAPTER REVIEW

Use the dictionary and thesaurus: Keep working with words and finding new and more accurate ways to express yourself.

When you can't call, write: Think of the pen as an extension of your newfound ability to speak out, and be heard.

Be curious about everything: Never stop asking questions. The facts you uncover enrich and enlighten everyday living. Everything's a learning experience.

Demand quality and service: Check out the warranties. Go to the ends of the earth (or write) to make them live up to their part of the bargain. Get what you pay for, and learn all you can about everything you observe.

That's living!

Notes and Observations

....

....

....

....

....

....

....

....

....

....

....

....

....

....

....

....

....

"Here's the Beef" shooting a Dinty Moore commercial in Culver City, CA, 1978

CHAPTER 7
"Actually it's Alfredo Sauce"

It was downright chilly that August morning as we left the mountain and entered the gently sloping valley of Kandersteg. The sun had just begun to warm away the mist that still hung at the base of that pyramid of ice and stone, and after camping that night on its slope, we were cold and hungry.

There is something about clean crisp mountain air, not to mention the exertion of climbing a 14,000 feet summit that piques the appetite, and that Swiss morning we were ravenous.

The breakfast we devoured in that small Kandersteg inn that fall morning is a meal I will never forget. Fresh eggs from the hen house out back, served sunny side up in their individual skillet placed hot on hollowed out bricks right at your table... huge terra-cotta mugs of hot milk, coffee and cocoa. The taste of rolls and croissants, still warm from the oven, with mounds of hand churned butter and piles of fresh fruit jam, is still in my mouth and on my mind.

In fact no single event stirs the imagination and sharpens the memory of past adventures, as much for me, as the incredible meals I have had in my travels. No bones about it, I love to eat.

The fact is, I put so much stock in a good meal, I won't let bad service stand in the way of its enjoyment.

It is one of the reasons I appreciate service in a restaurant, and why I demand it when it is lacking.

Unfortunately in today's fast paced society, service and quality are often not on the menu. Good food takes time. However even in the short order environment, your new found "mouth" can pay rich culinary dividends. First, if you have time to eat, you have time to **"Bitch"** if it is not to your liking.

Every "Haute Cuisine" devotee knows the time it takes time to properly prepare a meal, and the hours spent with cleaver and tongs in hand.

How many times do you remember your mother saying, "Don't eat so fast, I spent days on that meal"?

Of course restaurants have timesaving devices and their cooks know all the culinary short cuts, but in general, it takes more time to prepare a meal than we take to eat it.

There's a delightful scene from one of W.C. Fields movies where he goes into a diner to eat. Whatever he orders, it's either sold out, no longer on the menu, or not recommended by the waitress. In desperation, he finally asks for some water, only to find a bug in the dirty glass.

Even with the water shortages we have here in Los Angeles it's not quite that bad, but unless you stand up for service and the proper preparation of the food you order, it can sometimes seem so.

Through the years I have been lucky to be able to develop a fairly refined palate. In my travels I have been fortunate to eat in a few of the more famous restaurants in the world, when I could afford it.

I also found some of the best meals in little, out-of-the-way places. These were small family-owned businesses where everyone cared and was involved.

I'm sure you have your favorite spots and often order the same items off the menu, time and again, because you like how they are prepared and taste.

I'll try almost anything once, but I know what I like and I know how I like it. We have all been disappointed when ordering our favorite dish, only to discover that something is different.

Maybe the place has a new owner or the chef is sick, or worse, has just quit. Some might be willing to eat the food anyway, but not me, and I hope, not you. The food might be bad, but our "master mouth" is in good working order.

Even in the most unpretentious greasy spoons, fast food joints or cheap lunch counters, have you accepted less than you paid for? The eggs overdone, the toast burnt, or the coffee tasting like dishwater! (And that's just breakfast.)

Bad food and bad service can be found anywhere, from "Forget it" to "Four Seasons," from "Podunk" to "Paris." from "Hotels" to "Notells." But you don't have to take it.

There are the obvious exceptions. Dinner at the in-laws, when your girlfriend invites you to that first meal at her place, or when you personally do the cooking at yours.

One time I didn't have a choice comes to mind. Being big and strong, and a climber, I had been invited to join an expedition to Angel Falls, the highest waterfall in the world, at the headwaters of the Orinoco River in the Guiana Highlands of southeast Venezuela.

It seems that a flier named Jimmy Angel had discovered the falls in 1935 when looking for diamonds, and had crashed his plane, the Flamingo, while trying to land on the 4000 foot high plateau.

We were trying to get to the plane, and retrieve the note he'd left there twenty years before. It rained for three solid weeks and we never made it to the top of "Devil's Mountain." However the military junta in power at the time, in Caracas, gave us a particular farewell "state" dinner.

I'm not sure of the correct spelling, but it sounded like "Hiyucka," and believe me that's how it tasted. As we smiled for the cameras, they served us this special ceremonial dish.

It consisted of partially cooked eggs and meat, wrapped in banana leaves and stored underground in stone jars for a year. They were then excavated, steamed and served piping hot to us, as the news cameras rolled.

Can you imagine the odor that rose from those hot "rotten" banana leaves? As I said there are situations where you can't complain, but one of us did pass out.

Back in civilization, a dirty water glass doesn't seem so bad. Still, if you don't like the service or the food, you don't have to take it. Use your mouth, **"Bitch"** get what you want, the way you want it. <u>The way you deserve it.</u>

That is why I look forward to my once a week dinner gatherings with my friends Sterling and Bill. In an earlier chapter I mentioned we did a lot of verbal jousting together as we developed our "gift of gab" and challenged our minds and mouths.

Sterling is a master chef as well. Through the years he has whipped up some fantastic dishes, including the best mashed potatoes this side of Christendom.

All these years while proving a point, we have been passing the gravy. As we discussed our rights, we have been dishing out our cauliflower "au gratin." Between finding the flaws in each others philosophies, we have been discovering the slivers of garlic in the roast leg of lamb.

Recently in the middle of a heated discussion regarding my latest episode employing **"Bitch, Pitch and Get Rich,"** I made the mistake of asking one of them to pass the gravy. I was politely told, "Actually it's Alfredo Sauce." The point was made, and the "sauce" sure was tasty.

Thus we see again the value, yes, the **"Riches,"** of enduring friendships--learning and enriching life everyday by being involved through our curiosity, investigation and discovery.

CHAPTER REVIEW

Get what you pay for: Don't like the food? Send it back. Don't like the table? Move. Don't like the service? Tell the manager.

Enjoy the meal: If it's good, tell the server and the manager. Encourage excellence whenever you are lucky enough to find it. And tip accordingly.

Experiment: As in life, don't be afraid to try new things and new places. Variation adds spice and discovery to living. A great meal with friends. **Perfect!**

"Island at the Top of the World" shooting
at Disney Studios, Burbank, CA, 1974

CHAPTER 8

"Gold, not all that Glitters"

As we near the end of this book, doubtless some of you are wondering where is the chapter that contains the secret to the selection of the lotto numbers, or the pick six.

The title is **"Bitch, Pitch, and get Rich,"** *right?*

The point of this book is just to make money. *Not right!*

If you who are still looking for that one "magic answer" in these pages, perhaps you have missed the really important point. Is life only about wealth, or is it reaping the rewards that living has to offer every day?

Even Midas, in ancient Greek mythology, decided that for himself, when he washed away his powers in the Pactolur River. Everything he touched had turned to gold and gold is tough on the old choppers, not to mention being short on nutrition.

I sincerely hope by the time you finish reading this book, the entire import of this tome, (know the word?) will have become clear and meaningful.

Only by living life to the fullest, can we harvest the bounty, the **"Rich"**es that this brief existence offers. We can achieve our goals, fulfill our fantasies and realize our dreams at the same time.

If we get involved, stick our neck out, stand up and be counted, if we use the power of our newly developed "master mouth." if we **"Bitch,"**and **"Pitch,"** we will get **"Rich."**

But, not only with riches of the pocketbook, with riches of the spirit and the mind as well. To achieve the wondrous wealth that living has to offer we must start now, right away, while there is time. Life is so short. How quickly those 60 years between my fathers escapades and my own experiences flew by. Omar Khayyam, in his famous "Rubaiyat," said it far better than any of us could ever attempt to;

Come, fill the Cup, and in the Fire of Spring
The Winter Garment of Repentance fling;
The Bird of Time has but a little way To fly
And Lo! the Bird is on the wing.

When I came to Hollywood in the late sixties to be an actor in the movies, I joined the ranks of thousands that had come before. The lure and promise of fame and fortune had worked its magic on me, as on so many others.

I even thought the elusive dream of film immortality could be mine-- and the true magic is, it could still happen. As long as they keep playing reruns of shows like "Happy Days" or the old "Hawaii 5-0," I know I will be remembered.

The real lesson to be learned is that the riches of life are found on the road traveled, not in the ultimate destination.

After separating from the Air Force and leaving a remote base in King Salmon, Alaska, to find myself in the apparent civilization of Los Angeles, I needed to get a job. The path of life leads many ways.

I decide to take a part-time job at a classical sheet music store right on famous Hollywood Boulevard, called "DeKeyser Music." Here began an adventure in living, whose repercussions are still being felt by me today, over 45 years later.

Not only was Mr. DeKeyser one of the most memorable men I have met in my life, but the musical luminaries that came into his store, in the subsequent years were astounding . If you are into classical music, or Broadway musicals, you would have had been amazed.

John's store was the only serious sheet music store west of Chicago, and musicians, con- ductors and soloists from all over the world, came through the doors of that tiny shop.

But more than the music, it was the man himself. John DeKeyser had earned a repu- tation for knowing more about music pub- lished in the world than anyone else and his knowledge was incredible. Thus this little story fit into the book's theme of:

"Success at the tip of your Tongue"

First and foremost he had a work ethic second to none. He would spend months researching a rare piece of music for a customer regardless of their standing, be it a famous luminary or a beginning student.

Thinking only of his patrons, John was into customer service in a way that seems impos- sible today.

Even with all his hard work, he made what some might call a modest living, but he had the respect of the entire musical world.

One day a couple of slick wheeler-dealers from the East Coast came into the shop and button-holed Mr. DeKeyser, telling him how they could improve the efficiency of the store. They were going to do this and change that.

The store would double, triple its grosses. They had answers for everything. Every rebuttal was refuted, every statement was stymied, every question was answered, except one. John simply asked "What if I don't want any more money?" They didn't have an answer for that one.

They finally left the shop, shaking their heads and talking to themselves. It was inconceivable to them that anyone would not want to be **"Rich."** They had missed the point!

Mr. DeKeyser was **"Rich"**, beyond their ability to understand. He had enough money to live comfortably, but the totality of his wealth was not in coin, it was in the sum of those memories of all the wonderful people that had been touched by his kindness.

The sense of pride he felt by a lifetime of service, and above all, the literally thousands of individuals, both prominent and obscure, that were proud to call him a friend, was his enduring reward.

"Gold, not All that Glitters"

Talking of friends, from reading this book you know I am privileged to have been a small part of some truly wonderful and exciting peoples lives. Some have been extremely influential on a personal level, and others-- passing professional performers-- have, in the compressed reality of the performing world, left a brief but considerable impact on my life.

I'm sure if you give credit where credit is due, you will begin to realize how blessed you too have been with good friends, and how important and meaningful they have been in the forming of what other people know as **you**.

Pondering the passage of time and friends gone by in the winter of 1965, I wrote a piece entitled "The Traveler."

"The Traveler"

**A biting wind has caused his
lips to crack and ears now cherry red
have ceased to ache
His heavy steps lie trodden deep
upon the whitened path, as greying day
turns quickly into black.**

**The trail ahead both long and lean
with time now ever in the lead
Yet warm inside this traveler feels
as on he treks
for deep within he knows he walks with
friends.**

Hopefully you will agree that even this poetic digression has a place in a "how to" book that deals with the discovery and appreciation of life, as short as it is.

In **"Bitch, Pitch, and get Rich,"** we see the fine art of speaking your mind, of using your voice to not only be heard but heeded, is also the growth of all our faculties, as well as the fine tuning of our awareness of the world around us.

Let us look again at the path to verbal and personal success. This book has stressed conscious steps which, if followed and employed, will ensure individual growth, self-assurance, and great rewards.

Reread the chapters and start practicing the principles, and you will find, as I have found, these rewards in the continuing process:

1. Through curiosity about the language, we increase not only our vocabulary, but the practical use of these new

means of expression, to help us get our points across.

2. With practice and the trusty voice recorder we discover the expressiveness in our voice, and with it the power to persuade.

3. Honestly looking at ourselves, we challenge our willingness to speak the truth, supported by the facts.

4. Armed with the knowledge that when we do our best, we are the best, we have found new courage to speak our mind and our convictions.

5. By observing and questioning all we come in contact within our daily lives, we have been rewarded with understanding and the insights so enrich the quality of life.

6. Determining what we want and developing the courage to demand it from others, as well as ourselves, we have been afforded the quality and service we so richly deserve.

7. Realizing that as individuals, we can make a difference, we have begun to do battle against the careless indifference of the corporate mentality.

8. Knowing that success is achievable at every level, we are more willing to stick our necks out, risk being wrong, and learn from our mistakes.

9. And finally, we have come to understand that being **"Rich"** is more than just a pocket filled with gold, it is a mind filled with questions, an intellect filled with curiosity, a spirit filled with understanding, and a heart filled with the love of life.

These maxims, if followed, I firmly believe will make you richer than you ever thought possible. So at the end, we learn, **"Bitch, Pitch and get Rich"** is really just the beginning of the road that leads to living life.

One final story that links my father, the past, me, the present, and the essence of this final chapter,

"Gold, not All that Glitters."

Growing up in Brooklyn, we lived very near the Brooklyn Bridge. Two or three times a week the whole family would walk across the bridge to downtown Manhattan and have dinner at the "Automat" on Park Place.

The "Automat" was a great place to eat, especially for kids. With a hand full of nickels you could select what ever you wanted, put the money in the slot, turn the handle, the little glass door would pop open, and *Voila!* food.

On the way over and on the way back, as we traversed the bridge's promenade, my father would recite a poem. It was very long, especially for a little tike, but even then it interested me. The "Vagabond's House."

You already know my father's memory was such, that he knew it by heart, but without realizing it, I was learning it day by day. Twenty two stanzas, and before long I knew them all. To this day I still remember them, and those days on the bridge so long ago.

My first job in Hollywood, a quarter of a century later, was on the stage crew of a professional production of Edward Albee's play, "Tiny Alice" at the Ivar Theater.

We built a huge library set on the stage, the main set in the play. We ordered umpteen feet of used books to fill the walls of the set from floor to ceiling. Signe Hasso starred as Alice, and a great deal of the play's action took place in the library.

Filling the shelves took almost the whole day. Near the end I was surprised to find among the books I was putting on the highest shelf, a worn copy of Don Blanding's "Vagabond's House."

Once again a food of memories returned as I read the printed poem for the first time. It was exactly as my father had taught it to me, word for word, all those years ago.

Another ten years passed. I had loaned the book to friends, and in the interim, it had been lost, or just never returned. But I would still recite the poem now and again, from memory, to those who wanted to hear it.

Then one day, in the old "Hollywood Bookstore," on a small side street, Cherokee, I was looking for a book on Ancient Egypt, and there, in the wrong section, was the "Vagabond's House," a signed copy by the author, Don Blanding himself, in its 38th printing.

The faces of family and friends flashed in my mind, and I realized this book was an inseparable part of my life.

So it is with so many of the experiences of living. One thing leads to another and before you know it's a lifetime. Curiosity leads to interest, interest leads to questions, questions lead to answers, answers lead to solutions, solutions lead to success, and success hopefully leads to contentment.

It is not so much where you are going. Everyone who actually sees the top of the mountain, whether with their eyes, or in their mind, wants to get there. But it's the path taken to get there that counts.

One thing is certain, it is all in the experiences of the quest, and the people and places you pass along way. Perhaps, after you have seriously studied and applied the maxims this book shares, perhaps after you have lived a successful and productive life, perhaps after all is said and done you, like me, will see and agree that living life to the fullest was, and is, the ultimate achievement, and in itself the true wealth living has to offer.

Finally, I would like to share with you a poem from that book, found, lost and found again, Don Blanding's "Vagabond's House" and his idea (and mine, and after reading this book, hopefully yours) of what it is to be truly **"Rich."**

GOLD

**My treasure chest is filled with gold.
Gold...gold...gold.
Vagabond's gold and drifter's gold...**

**Worthless, priceless dreamer's gold,..
Gold of the sunset...gold of the dawn...
Gold of the shower trees on my lawn...
Poet's gold and artist's gold...
Gold that can not be bought or sold...**

Gold

Remember, you only pass this way once. You owe it to yourself and all who love you and care about you to truly live life to the fullest.

Maximize your potential by looking in the mirror every day, and saying out loud, I will not cheat myself of the joys life has to offer. I will work to make myself better every day and look for the best in myself and others.

And when you need some help along life's path, stand tall, smile and simply:

"BITCH, PITCH and get RICH"

Lee Paul

The tall one, in Pi Epsilon Tau (National Petroleum Honorary) Marietta College, 1958

"Theater in the Park" troupe with John Hillerman, and a man with a pipe, 1960

On location for "Movie of the Week" Condominium Panama City Beach, FL, 1980

Another "Bad Guy" trying to "Survive Game" on location, Aptos, CA, 1987

Lee Paul

"A Perfect Party" at the Richard Basehart Theater in Los Angeles with H.M. Wynant, 1988

Ready to visit Venice, and Saint Mark's
Square via the Carnival Liberty, circa 2006

The warmth of sun on the Rivera, at "Monte
Carlo" via the Carnival Liberty, circa 2006

Kathy and I, and "The Titanic Grand Staircase"
on the Carnival Pride, circa 2004

Lee Paul

Notes and Observations

Notes and Observations

....

....

....

....

....

....

....

....

....

....

....

....

....

....

....

....